C000269839

Songs of the Vagabond

John Bradburne

Selected and edited by David Crystal

Holy Island Press

First published in 1996 by
Holy Island Press
PO Box 5
Holyhead
Gwynedd LL65 1RG, UK

© The John Bradburne Memorial Society
Brick House, Risbury, Leominster HR6 0NQ, UK

Printed by W O Jones (Printers Ltd), Llangefni, LL77 7EH, UK

All rights reserved. No part of this publication may
be reproduced, stored in a retrieval system, or
transmited, in any form or by any means,
electronic, mechanical, photocopying, recording, or
otherwise, without the prior permission of the
John Bradburne Memorial Society.

British Library Cataloguing in Publication Data

A catalogue record for this book
is available from the British Library.

ISBN 0 9513063 4 0

The front cover shows a woodcut, designed by a monk of Buckfast Abbey, of John Bradburne's hermitage in Mutemwa, Zimbabwe, with Chigona hill in the background. The back cover photograph is of John Bradburne inside his hut, at his typewriter.

Contents

John Bradburne (1921—1979)

John Randal Bradburne was born at Skirwith, Cumbria, the son of an Anglican clergyman. After secondary school in Norfolk, he joined the army in 1939, and served in Malaya and Burma, before being invalided home. Something in Malaya - a Pauline experience, it is said - turned him from adventurer into pilgrim.

He became a Roman Catholic in 1947 when staying at Buckfast Abbey. After some months with the Carthusians, he felt the urge to travel, and for 16 years wandered between England, Italy, and the Middle East, living out of a Gladstone bag. Then he wrote to his friend Father John Dove in Zimbabwe asking 'Is there a cave in Africa where I can pray?'

Soon after his arrival, in 1962, he confided to a Franciscan priest that he had three wishes: to serve leprosy patients, to die a martyr, and to be buried in the habit of St Francis.

From 1964 he was caretaker of a new centre near Harare. Then in 1969 he was appointed warden of Mutemwa Leprosy Settlemernt, near Mutoko, Zimbabwe. His first wish.

The single-minded loving care he gave his patients eventually brought him into conflict with the management committee, and he was sacked. He then lived in a prefab tin hut, lacking water and sanitation, just outside the leprosy compound. From there this 'strange vagabond', as he often called himself, continued to help them as much as he could.

As a lay member of the Third Order of St Francis, he obeyed its rule, singing the daily office of Our Lady. He lived its hours, rising at dawn for Matins and ending the day with Vespers and Compline. This discipline provides the context for many poems, written at the turning-points of the day.

During the Zimbabwean civil war, his efforts to prevent the exploitation of the patients brought local hostility and suspicion. He was taken by guerrillas, and shot – on Wednesday, 5 September. A line of poetry reads: 'Come sweet death on Wednesday, if you will and if you may'. His second wish.

At his Requiem Mass, eye-witnesses saw three drops of blood fall from the bottom of the coffin, forming a little pool on the ground. The coffin was re-opened, but no sign of blood was found. However, it was noticed that he had been buried in a shirt. It was replaced by the Franciscan habit. His third wish.

Since his death, many unusual events have been reported in relation to his name. His monument at Mutemwa is now a place of pilgrimage, and there is a growing movement to recognise him as Zimbabwe's first saint. This is the context which has prompted the publication of the present book.

Dates of the poems

I *Gay matter for a graying mattoid* 9 Jul 1978; *If only I had the time* 14 Feb 1978; *Talisman* 5 Mar 1969
II *Reminiscence* 20 Aug 1971; *Ad tertiam / sextam / nonam* 29 Jan 1970; *Avon's above* 2 Jul 1969; *Overflow* 25 Mar 1969; *Revels* Aug 1971; *Aubade* March 1969; *A ballade of a rectory garden* 7 Apr 1975; *To the Fairy Queen* 20 Jul 1978; *Lauds on Ladyday* 25 Mar 1969; *Greensleeves* 24 Sep 1973
III *Spring is in the air* 21 Jul 1978; *For a peal of eight* 6 Mar 1978; *Cogito* 26 Aug 1973; *Ad completorium* 26 Aug 1973; *Sheer prestige* 22 Jan 1975; *Discretion* 31 Aug 1973
IV *Come follow* 18 Mar 1973; *Love* 22 Sep 1971; *Ad Mariam* 14 Jun 1978; *Steep gradient* 26 Apr 1969
V *Alma mater* 1 Apr 1969; *Excelsior* 20 Aug 1971; *Ritornello* 28 May 1978; *Idyll of the spring* 27 Jan 1969; *In magno silentio* 28 May 1978; *Salve, San Antonio* 13 Feb 1970 ('Hail, St Anthony'); *God shave the Queen* 30 May 1978
VI *Ornithological images* 28 Aug 1973; *Of swans* 22 Feb 1978; *Here and there* 13 Mar 1978; *Of ravens* 23 Feb 1978; *Second vespers* Jan 1978; *Prime* 11 Oct 1971; *Nascent apiary* 21 Jul 1973; *Nocturne* 22 Jul 1973; *Quis ut Deus* 15 Sep 1971
VII *A ballad of an ancient usher* 16 Feb 1978; *Aubade* Mar 1971; *On the feast of Corpus Christi* 28 May 1978; *Cryptic chaplets* 15 Aug 1978; *Meridian* 24 Feb 1978; *A Christmas message* May 1978
VIII *In principio* 24 Aug 1973; *Brewing* 30 Oct 1978; *Untearfully at tierce* 29 May 1978; *Quid nunc?* Aug 1971 *Ad tertiam* 15 Mar 1971
IX *Chigona* 27 Aug 1973; *By moonlight* 6/7 Oct 1973; *Kraaldom* Aug 1971; *Little world of Dunlopillo* 19 Feb 1970; *Momento Kahoto* 8 Jun 1978; *Josephite* 30 Jan 1970; *Paradise tossed aside* Aug 1978
X *Beedom attained* 14 Aug 1973

Preface

John Bradburne breathed poetry. It came out of him like water from a tap - and the tap was always on. The climax of a remarkable poetic life, which began in his youth, was the decade from 1969, when he wrote some 6,000 poems - sometimes a dozen or more in a day. As one would expect, with such a remarkable outpouring, the quality varies enormously, from the sublime to the banale, but his work throughout displays a single-minded enthusiasm and clarity of vision that is compelling in its intensity and endearing in its humanity.

Metaphors of breathing and outpouring were never more apt than in the case of John Bradburne. On the 20th of April 1969 he begins a letter home from what was then Salisbury, Rhodesia:

> Dearest Mother, many thanks for your three last letters: of the 9th, of the 12th and of the 15th. Writing in anything other than verse is to me a sterile, fruitless and abortive pain, so I am sure you will allow me the pleasure of replying in verse and in verse of giving you what news and Paschaltidings I may have. In saying that writing in anything other than verse is to me heaviness, I do not refer to what I receive but to what I send.

He then launches exuberantly into a poem of over 100 lines, in which joyful romanticism and domestic chat are obliviously juxtaposed:

> It makes me happy and augments my glees
> To read about the pleasure which you had
> In Paschal greetings on Masasa trees
> The sight of which in Spring makes many glad;
> Bless-ed be God that Allelulias leapt
> To Easter sunshine best of twenty years,
> Receded winter cold, no longer slept
> The daffodils but trumpeted their cheers!
> Hurrah for Mary gladdened in the way
> With Auriol on Easter holiday.
>
> Such marked improvement in the health of him
> Whose name is Charles (which rhymes with nothing well)
> Is also Alleluiattic, swim
> May he this Summer, sound as any bell ...

His best work contains lines of great beauty and profound spiritual insight. Many of his images are original and vivid:

Adhere to Truth as flies do to the ceiling ...

The Thought of God is written in the air ...

He can produce romantic images of startling quality, inviting comparison with Robert Browning or William Blake.

Dreams are a chequered commentary made
In sleep along the deeps of our desires
Moving like riddles through a magic glade
Lightly they touch the leap of hidden fires ...
(From 'Come Follow' (*not in this collection*))

He looks at nature in ways that Wordsworth or Keats would have been proud of. Here is an image of bees:

The night-sound of a hive is like the fall
Of fairy raindrops on the tops of time ...

And one of ravens:

Ravens are Yahweh's craftiness with wings ...

And one of swans:

Companiable not, as ships that sail alone
With unhailed mast upon the vast unchartered seas
So is the single solitary swan to own
Tis never less alone, O Lord, than, throned with Thee,
Upon a pilgrimage where none but One can be.

And here is an atmospheric narrative opening:

There's a long dark wood where the witches dwell
By a marsh where the curlews call
And above and beyond there is conned a Fell
Whence a Wind doth the dales befall ...

What makes John Bradburne special as a poet is his mastery of the traditional features of verse: onomatopoeia, verbal allusion, rhythm, and rhyme. He experiments with every conceivable metre. No blank verse for him:

If only you had time for writing verse?
True poets have got time for nothing less!
Vers libre I am consigning to its hearse,
With rhyme and rhythm onward John will press!

He wants to 'weave with rhyme' – though he can produce a free
verse style when he wants to – but his rhymes are not restricted
to the ends of lines. He glories in rhyming words within lines,
using alliteration and assonance.

Take tower, turrets, copper-beeches, aisles
And roses, rows of reverential yews
And lilac and laburnum and the smiles
Of Maytime married to the chiming views
Of swallowdom and cuckomerry mews ...

He can take alliteration to almost tongue-twisting lengths:

First Eve fell fast for fallen fiend's false fable ...

Words resonate against each other in unexpected ways. They
are probed, twisted, stretched, and pummelled, to yield every
ounce of structure and connotation. Bradburne's poetry is a
punster's paradise.

Yield, thou letter last but one,
On Alpha bet
As being Omega's own Son
And End shall never set:
Give, vibrate, penultimate,
Till all is Zed and done save Zen ...

He is obsessed with word-play and allusion, and he knows it,
calling himself rhymster and punster in mock self-
disparagement. I doubt whether anyone could wring more
linguistic changes out of a word: Eve, Eva, Ave, Mary, Maria,
mare, au mer, Miriam, Admire I Am ... And he is always ready
to play, as in this extract from 'Cosmic Cogitations' (not in this
collection):

A is for Apple,
B is for Beads.
C is for counting them,
D is for deeds,
E is for ecstasy,

F is for flight,
G is for Gabriel coming by night
H is for happiness,
I is for ink,
J is for jotting what is not too dotty to think ...

It is this pervasive playfulness which prevents his poetry from becoming pompous or self-indulgent. He has only one theme, and it is the most profound of themes: the nature of the triune God, as manifested in Jesus, as born of Mary. From this theme come all others - God's plan in human history, salvation, love, mission ... Bradburne gets as close as he can to the godhead, through the figure of Mary. He sees himself as in the most daring and intimate of relationships to her, as one 'married to the Queen of Queens'. In his vision, all insights and images come directly from her:

This day thy Queen conceived God's word by Me.

In such a night as this I know
That what I say she says is so.

And his insights are profound - at times mystical to the point of obscurity, at times burning with prophetic clarity, as in this brilliant image of the Trinity:

Love who is Chooser, Chosen, Choice.

John Bradburne is nonetheless a very human poet. He does not hide his own fears and failings. When his temper gets the better of him, and he treats an unwanted visitor badly, he condemns himself later that evening in a poem. He has good days and bad days: 18 August 1971 was a bad day, and is punished by being sent to bed without any poetry:

Numbers this day amongst the very worst
I've had: sad, it shall not be further versed.

And although he often writes at all hours of the night, he finds it difficult to get up in the morning:

After first cockcrow while the late owls cry
And stilly crickets chirp the way to dawn
Ripe is the time to type that poetry
Which stole upon one long before the morn

And got itself imprinted on the mind
Yet seldom then I rise with yen, I find!

These flashes of everyday humanity show John Bradburne to be
no ordinary Romantic. Do we know from their poems whether
Keats or Coleridge found it difficult to get up in the morning?

Many of Bradburne's poems are flawed in their total structure.
In the very long works (of hundreds of lines - not represented in
this collection), the organization can break down completely,
and one is carried along by the force of individual verses not
knowing where the story will end. Despite their intended
metrical discipline, lines sometimes do not scan, and verses
become unsymmetrical. But none of this seemed to bother him.
He laughs at his own inability to find a rhyme, and if the last
line of a poem isn't right, he leaves it be, often adding a jocular
footnote to draw attention to the point. There is very little sign
of self-correction in the original typescripts and manuscripts.
As the thought came to mind, so he put it down, at speed and
without hesitation, in usually impeccable verse.

We never stop to wonder what to say,
The impetus of our committing muse
Imprisons us in fairy-spells that sway
Whichever rhyme and rhythm she may choose ...

With such aninspiration, there was no need for revision - and
anyway, there was no time, for the next poem had to be written.

Six thouand poems. Why did he do it? Did he have a choice?
'Bards are birds', he says in 'Talisman':

Birds that spontaneously sing
Ask not reward or anything
Of man's appreciation, they
Being but God's make songs each day
Especially at morn and eve:
In giving thanks they thanks receive.

But in 'Paradise tossed aside' we finally come closer to an
understanding of the mission of this 'strange vagabond':

... oh may this dunce's typing
Re-stir the springs of immortality
And may my wit befit eternity.

I   *Weaving rhymes*

Gay matter for a graying mattoid

If they should pick me off tonight
And leave me on the floor
I'd pray before my soul took flight
That all this heretofore
Of reams and reams of nursery-rhymes
Might be well sorted out betimes
And not be published where it chimes
Not in with sinless lore.

I pray that all its flaws may be
Erased by some good friend for me
If I'm left not the time to see
It sorted to the core ...
But this I'm sure about: it lacks
Nor charms nor farms nor psalms in stacks
And this Immaculately backs

If only I had the time

If only you had time for writing verse?
True poets have got time for nothing less!
Vers libre I am consigning to its hearse,
With rhyme and rhythm onward John will press!
Blank verse can go and swank to cranky pedants
And rank itself as genius at war
With genius! we rhymsters are the presents
Of God Most High to boredom on the floor!
Remark our exclamation-marks successive
And say they are excessive if you will,
We simply love to be so retrogressive
As reckons Nursery-rhyme sublimest still:
    We like to weave with rhyming, in and out
    The golden thread goes through, undoing doubt.

We never stop to wonder what to say,
The impetus of our committing muse
Imprisons us in fairy-spells that sway
Whichever rhyme and rhythm she may choose;
Mistressed amidst this cosmic influence
We utterly abandon to her power
The whole expression of our song and dance
Which merges with the sunshine and the shower;
Blest are the seasons while this Nurserymaid
Aids and abets us and directs our themes
And she is very gracefully arrayed
To nurse our verses, none the worse for dreams:
    Without two banks what stream will reach the ocean?
    Between both rhyme and metre fleet's our motion.

Talisman

Birds that spontaneously sing
Ask not reward or anything
Of man's appreciation, they
Being but God's make songs each day
Especially at morn and eve:
In giving thanks they thanks receive.

Lord, I would ask it now this morn,
No other task but, unforlorn
From lack of mortal praise of what
I need to write for lucre not
I may continue, morn and eve,
Songs that Our Lady may receive.

Indeed no other task I wish,
Neither to hunt or shoot or fish
For pleasure, all my pleasure is
In offering these oddities
To God's good Mother; Second Eve,
Adamant I, my songs receive!

Though I might go and wonders work
Amongst the sick, this would I shirk
Openly only that I may
Make songs of beauty each new day:
Sweet Mistress mine, but make-believe
Were occupation else, I cleave.

'This day I make you this reply,
Leave all to me for you can fly
Quite like a swallow, skim with words
The deeps and shallows; bards are birds
And here and now these lines believe
Leaders to readers will receive'.

II   *Wearing Mary*

Reminiscence

I passed through France when all her corn
Stood stooked and booked in golden sheaves
For harvest-home; no Roman born,
I was and am that ass believes
In Mass and Eucharist as means
Of marrying the Queen of Queens ...

But formally I married her
(Whom mystically may
   Any she'll ask and well prefer)
In Italy one day:
Before the dawn and long before
I climbed a hill, declined to snore,
Ascending on a winding road
Midst vines and olives barely showed
Till glowed the dawn and gleamed the East ...
Then fairness of Campania increased
Before my gladdened sight; and in I went
To ancient church for my great Patron meant:
Into the Baptist's church at high Castello
Di Palma, and he said, 'Well wed, young fellow!'.

Ad tertiam

My wife is fair, lovely beyond all others,
To her I'd hark, more to endorse my love,
In anything she wanted, nothing smothers
The fact that she is with me whilst above;
Each morning I may clearly read her thoughts
Writ in Epistle and Gospel for the day
And, while I freely read, her Truth supports
My meditation and directs my way;
She's not so mild and meek as cannot oust
And utterly surpass the wildest beauty,
She is my mount on which I ride to joust,
Lightly caparisoned she bears to duty:
She raises me from every dazing fall
With, 'Nay, it was no nightmare after all!'.

Ad sextam

Mine Ark is dark within but beautiful,
She sails supreme e'en where the passions heave,
When anger roars upon me like a bull
Or like a lion ramps, she bids me weave;
A little while I weave in words and then
Feel well despite the swelling of the waves,
My loom's a typewriter, my ready Pen
Sails like a Queenly Swan whose King-Cob saves;
The maize before my door in summer sun
Grows daily higher and the lands are green,
He knows (who is Maria's Holy One)
How best from worldly restlessness to wean:
By means of her who is both Mother, Bride
And daughter blest of God He rules the tide.

Ad nonam

So, we proceed towards our holy land
And go a-jogging on in rustic joy
To temporary solace, gorge is spanned,
The George and Dragon Inn befits our ploy;
I do not know if any reader will
Believe me when I say the Barmaid is
Emmanuel's own Mother or that he
Is here Mine Host, who fears for heresies?
Moreover, there's a parrot in a state
Of perfect freedom in this very House
Repeating aye, as if to celebrate
The Lord of wine divine who bids carouse,
'Shalom, Shalom, Shalom!': and that is all
The greeting here you'll get to cheer your call.

Avon's above

I think the liquefaction of the wave,
The shimmering of lake and lily-pool,
Are like my queen's attraction to her knave
As elementally she laves her fool;
Reflecting on the flow and in the still
She steals amidst the mirror of my mind,
Completely mistresses and sweetly till,
Fair Lady playing cool, I'm tool resigned;
Then art thou Pen, and I thy cygnet-cob
And simply nib that fills from fount of thine,
Over the page thou glidest, guide the job
Thou and the passion ford to sward ashine
Quickly! (I saw my merry Wife upon
The waters moving, proving like a Swan).

Overflow

The plenitude of spirit overflows,
The martial eagle stoops from out the blue,
The fattened steer amidst the fastness lows,
Slowly the sun mounts up to zenith true;
Soon beeves go gather to the random glade
And clump together in the silvan cool,
Grasshoppers cling, like halcyon arrayed,
To golden nectar-cups nigh lily-pool;
Wallow my dogs in water while I sit
Watching the mighty wheeling of a pair
Of secretary-birds which well befit
The Spirit of the Lord who writes on air:
I AM wide-wing'd and wild and wondous free,
This day thy Queen conceived God's word by Me.

Revels

Rolling babes or strolling players,
Clinging near or flinging far,
Crawling pubwise, taxi-payers,
Barmaid hail as Morning Star:
Search whatever hour you're at
The Church I'm in, free habitat.

Rise and shine with wine-red noses,
Go to sleep with glowing hearts,
Life can be a bed of roses
If God's wife directs your parts:
Sufferings and passing troubles
Are outclassed by joy that bubbles.

Fools immortal, portal enter
Whence was born our Lord and King,
Make our Lady's womb your centre
For delight in each right thing:
Moon and sun and stars gyrating
Fete this boon of graceful gating.

Chain yourselves to elves' gay Ruler
Tied to Mary's apron-strings
Gallant grows the whilom drooler,
Erstwhile knaves take style of kings:
Willy-nilly bards become
Great if in her gait they strum.

Sways the hip and slips the texture,
Liquefaction is her art,
Queen Immaculate won't lecture
Like a prude once wooed your heart:
Rally in this gown of glory,
Wearing Mary is my story.

'Wearing Mary nearly out
Is this clearly forward scout!'.

Aubade

In mists, the middle distance seems a sea
Out which rise highlands like the Isles of Greece,
The dawn adores and argent is the glee
Of all that valley with its veiling fleece;
Easterly looking, marvel at the sight
And read the book of glory open there
Where lowliness, veiled over in the white
Ocean of morning mists, is hid as fair;
Descry the little hills of conelike shape,
Behold those mightier, each lifts its head
As giant that already breasts the tape
Into the heavens, glowing gold and red:
This is Palm Sunday, dawn's inaugural psalm
Dame Nature raises to her Lord of charm.

Calm are the tidings of that argent sea
And she whose name embraces all The Seven
(Meaning Maria) beckons Easterly
And indicates my earthly route to Heaven;
Did I not wish for Oriental flavour
Of suffering as mute as lepers know
Being so powerless in frames, that waver
Diminishing, as limb by limb they go?
Did I not wish to share in beggar's choice
Of having none beneath the sun to count
Him anything of earthly worth? rejoice
If there disdain shall grow and scorn shall mount
For thee (Maria whispers as the mist
Disperses and my verse is being kissed).

Palm Sunday 1969

A ballade of a rectory garden

Take towers, turrets, copper-beeches, aisles
And roses, rows of reverential yews
And lilac and laburnum and the smiles
Of Maytime married to the chiming views
Of swallowdom and cuckoomerry mews,
And harness them together in a train
Of thought that runs from fountain-upon-Muse
Infusing wine, not water, into brain.

Brain takes it in and Aubrey beams, beguiles
Both lilies gay and Galilean views
With something like a symphony of miles
And miles of hilltops hopping to the News
Which is the Gospel-Truth: then, all those pews
Of swank and all those ranks of chairs, that gain
No grace for congregations, face my Muse
Infusing wine, not water, into brain.

The oddness of God's airy-fairy styles
gets even with the echoes that enthuse
As, underneath that hayrick which beguiles
My head by being hair, the mountain-views
Marry the rolling panoramas, fuse ...
My mouth is as an organ not in vain
Made vibrant by the South-West Wind: my Muse
Infusing wine, not water, into brain.

Envoi

Prince, the dayenewehmont: above the yews
Amidst a copper-beechen crown I reign
Playing a mouth-organ ... La Reine ma Muse
Infusing wine, not water, into brain.

To the Fairy Queen

Shall all my stuff and nonsense stay
Intact until my dying day?
Fair Lady, Fairy Queen, do say ...
'Indeed, indeed, and Yes!'.

Nonsense and stuff I dedicate
To thee, sweet Queen Immaculate
I hope and trust that Heaven's Gate
Will cope with it: 'We shall!
My gait will swing and I will dance
To Honi soit qui mal y pense!'.

In such a night as this I know
That what I say she says is so.

'Fiat!'.

Lauds on Ladyday

The angel of the Lord
Unto Miriam declared
And the saying brought accord
On an answer unimpaired
To the air, to the earth,
To the water and the fire
And the elemental worth
Stood attuned to desire
Like a lyre new-strung
And the singing of the rills
Was as lyrical a tongue
As the springs in the hills.

Little Galilean boats
Of the fishers in the night
Went a-dipping in the gloats
Of the wavelets light
And the Lily gay replied
To the great annunciation
'Be it done' and the bride
Is to every generation
Named the Blest, and the glee
Of the vale and the plain
Runs West to the sea
And to Galilee again.

While the stars looked down
And the earth looked up
Shone below a chosen town,
Shone above a loving-cup
And the Trinity sat drinking
In the deeps of a still
Linked up with the thinking
Of the Father as, athrill,
The Word leapt fast
To the womb and the mould
And the Grail and the cast
And the House of Gold.

Greensleeves

It is important for a man
Who lives alone with love of God
To honour the monastic plan
In spite of no abbatial rod.

The more his mind's to keep his cell
The more he finds that dwelling gay,
If he has learnt to weigh it well
'El' will be all he'll need to pray.

But whosoever lives alone
With love of God must also love
His Mother – Queen upon the throne
Of hearts she cleans and weans above.

Green-sleeved are all the avenues
From English Spring to Spring at hand,
In jacarandas too my Muse
Delights in this Mashonaland.

No exile in the land of Ham
I sing the song that rang along to Walsingham.

III   *Chooser, Chosen, Choice*

Spring is in the air

The Thought of God is written in the air,
Weather and wind express Him with His Word,
Behold the hills so high above low care
And hark to Yahweh's Voice in larksong heard;
The Thought of God is God The Father good,
The Word of God expresses what God thinks,
The Voice of God wings vibrant in the wood
Singing, or in our hearts with silence links;
These Three are Love Begetting, Love Begotten
And Love Proceeding as The Voice of both,
Love is Our God and King and nothing loth
To sink into the silence, unforgotten:
    Switch off that Radio, it rots the scene,
    Besets our souls that Television Screen!

For a peal of eight

An eastern isle of untold charm
Was once bombarded from the sea
With such an occidental psalm
That it was much upset like thee
Being informed that Yahweh's Three
Persons are Thought and Word and Voice
Of One Sole Substance which is Free
Love who is Chooser, Chosen, Choice.

Begetting Love is Father calm,
Begotten Love His Son is He
And Love Proceeding like a psalm
Is Charmer of Saint Peter's See
Who haunts it with His Melody
Singing The Thought, The Word, The Voice
Of which all knowledge has one She
Love who is Chooser, Chosen, Choice.

For appeal of eight times more alarm
Than Queen of Sheba had stands She
Who is the Queen of grace and charm
And Carmel, and of Persons Three
The Daughter, Mother and most free
Mistress that ever was in voice
Tuned to turn the atoneing Key
Love who is Chooser, Chosen, Choice.

Envoi
Prince, saunter up and down with me
And bid the cruiser's crew rejoice
Upon arriving at the Quay:
Love who is Chooser, Chosen, Choice.

Cogito

Unimaginary image
Of the Father and the Son
And the Spirit fits the page:
Mind, Will, Memory – at one.

Memory befits the Father,
Mind we find befits the Son,
Will befits the Spirit rather
Than another of The One.

In the One is not another
Any of the Three than Love:
Love Begotten is our Brother,
Love Proceeding is the Dove.

Love Begetting from all ages
Is the Father of the Word:
Runs the Thought through all the stages
Of the Voice whose choice is heard.

Heard from Rome when God announces
Through the Pope, a mortal man,
What He wills; it stills; it bounces
Back through the Prophetic plan.

While the Word, the walking Yahweh,
Went through Galilee and taught,
Blithesome birds and lilies gay
Hailed His Father of the Thought.

Thoughts are fathered oft by wishes,
Wishes sired by inward flame;
Brittle gods and little fishes
All gave way to Yahweh's claim.

Mind, by mind, unmediaeval,
Mean I not the memory
But the intellect we call
The understanding faculty.

Treating of the Triune image
Of the Lord amidst the soul
We reflect upon the message
Of His Mind Incarnate, whole.

In the Mind, in Christ our Maker,
We behold the Father's thought
Which can never be forsaker
Of the Word: expression wrought.

Breakers from the Father's thinking
Hit the lands by Christ the Word
But the Ship is never sinking
And the Helmsman's Voice is heard.

In the Memory however
We reflect the Father Most:
Back and back it goes to sever
Never from the Son, Mine Host.

See Him at the sacred table,
Recognize Him in the Mass:
This the spirit will enable,
Well's the will that is His glass.

Human father, human son
Certainly are not but one;
Human perfectly, Divine
Perfectly, The Son doth shine
One with the Father: God! (Odd final line).

Ad completorium

I'll not forget this day
So long as I may live,
Never a better lay
To me did Yahweh give
Than 'Cogito': I think
And therefore am alive
To the fact that at the brink
Of eternity should strive
Each Christian soul to stand
A-tiptoe on God's hand.

Sheer prestige

At gradient of One in Three we climb
Up Porlock pulling forelocks to the Lord
Who is the Author of that book sublime
Expressing Yahweh's Thought, home and abroad;
Call it a chess board if you like the game,
The partridges and pheasants will advance
Beyond the coverts in a quest for fame
Which is as wild as violets in France;
Take any turn you fancy after that
Or travel the Sahara in a yacht
But don't forget to raise your bowler-hat
To God The Voice, the choicest Polyglot:
    Word of The Father Thought, art Thou above
    Better unfurled than in this world we love?

Discretion

I grappled with The Trinity
Till Saint Augustine said,
'You'd better stop, God's Mystery
Is bigger than man's head!':
Hugging the doctor's good advice
With a mug of tea was very nice.

IV Dreams and desires

Come follow

Dreams are a chequered commentary made
In sleep along the deeps of our desires,
Moving like riddles through a magic glade
Lightly they touch the leap of hidden fires;
Yielding to fickle fancy's custom, dreams
Pursue impossibilities with zest,
Essentially ephemeral their themes
Recount us for the worst or for the best;
Clarity oft they lack, disparagement
Enters their border softly as they part,
Indeed they feed upon defeat's intent
Vying for victory amidst the heart:
    Ensured by dreams some gleaming schemes come true
    Divinely from a human follow-through.

Love

Love is a short disease, a long desire,
A strong and lasting healing; love is like
An angler landing fish, a hand at lyre,
A roadhog flogging home his motor-bike;
Love is a deep unsleeping thing, leaps time
And steeps amidst eternity for rest
And love is like three candles lighting rhyme
And metre I am making for the best;
An Alleluiatic sequence shows
A little of love's eloquence that lasts;
Love has three lights, one to another glows,
A third proceeds between: naught overcasts
True love because it knows that it possesses,
Being possessed, a zest above distresses.

O as to the caress of lightsome love
Steady as is unflickering a flame
No less is human that than is above
Proud condescension one Divine we claim;
The flame goes out alone to throne the fire
Of three that shall not ever be put out
Even by my shortcoming in desire
Not yet perpetual, beset by doubt;
No mortal man should ever be retired
From obligation to proceed in joy
With loving since by loving he was sired
And love may be immortally his ploy:
    As honey is the sweetness of the bees
    And wax the sealing of it, love doth please ...
    And both can melt and so may hearts, with ease!

Ad Mariam
To the mare
Ad mare

Not vainly in a reminiscent vein
As year succeeds to year we make refrain
But if we will refrain from thinking back
There gains on us The Witchwood: was it black?

There's a long dark wood where the witches dwell
By a marsh where the curlews call
And above and beyond there is conned a Fell
Whence a Wind doth the dales befall:
Its name is The Helm and it hurls down hard
On the strong sequestered farm and the yard
And it well may break that gate five-barred
And it batters the granite wall.

Though the Evening Star may brightly shine
While will-o-the-wisps conspire
Boldly to shoot a homely line
With an incandescent fire,
The gnomes and the trolls and the goblins know
When the hellish Helm will wish to blow
Burlyly out and down to below
To belabour the nave and the choir!

But soft, far off from Cumberland
In the mellower realm of York
Stood there a saint who still may stand
With the shades in the cloister-walk:
Archbishop he of the See well-known
As second to Cantaur alone
But they begged him come and leave his throne
That fiendish Helm to baulk.

O'er hill and dale Paulinus strode,
If he rode twas on an ass...
He stopped with charm at the charmed abode
And in via said clearly Mass:
He came at last to the Bottoms long
Of the Pennine Chain than Rome more strong
In matters temporal of the throng
Of the Legions ... Legions pass.

He climbed to the height of that highest Fell
And he bid that demon Go!
He signed the height with the Sign known well
As the Sign of the Cross, and so
Crossfell was called itself, baptised
Whence the fiend, compelled to, realized
That his day was done... was none surprised
When again The Helm did blow?

Not you, not I, our home was there
In sight of the rainbowed Fell,
Nursery-games went free of care,
Went calling names as well!
But I who have no bottom much
Am called Fell-Bottom, such-and-such
And bubbling bard whose double-dutch
Is Heaven's, not of hell.

Still the Witchwood stands where stand it did
And the foxgloves grow where the Parson bid:
In case his name's remaining hid
Draws Broadstream Eden up the lid
And flows down thence au mer!

Steep gradient

Who'll be faithful in the battle, valiant amidst the fray,
If amongst his peaceful cattle never stood he strong a day?
If in piping times of plenty never school we for the hard –
When the foes get sniping, sentry, back we inch and then a yard:
Inch by inch we go to flinching, ounce by ounce grows body fat,
Now's the time sublime for winning! willing winch, well govern that.

Up, my spirit, wind my working round the windlass of the will,
Wheel about upon the shirking, bid the shifty sense be still!
How, if now I train in nothing, fit my wits for famine not,
Shall I stand when earth is quaking, shaking what I thought my plot?
Four square meals a day and later, six full feet beneath the ground,
Shall I find me heaven's hater or equated to the crowned?

Joys, go sorrow! toy's tomorrow, silly thing ungripped thou art
Futile, Future! Now's my suitor, now I'll woo with all my heart!
Dame is fortune, fortune's woman, flee her for a faithless jade,
Fast will follow joy on sorrow, wed the present undismayed:
Surely fortune's like a shadow, I'll be runner in the Sun
And she'll follow like a swallow, migrant, to the Three in One.

V Haunted by God

Alma mater

I am as uncompetitive a man
As ever failed to grace a first fifteen,
I never seemed to leave where I began –
Climbing the trees to height sublimely green;
I thought the Sports Field less befitted Cricket
In Summertime than humming in the deep
By bees whilst fell, first ball, my middle wicket
At which cheered grasshoppers with every leap;
Meseemed the boundary should be attained
Not by the ball but more by me and crossed
For reaching fields afar and woods where reigned
They who achieved tree-crowns in breezes tossed:
Am I support to Darwin in his theory
Upon our antecedents? just a query.

The naming of my schoolplace meant a Wood,
In Chaucer you will find that word of Holt,
Well memorize that Prologue once I could
Though never in Eleven called a Colt;
'Dolt' (by renewal after old Headmaster)
I clearly can remember me addressed
When mathematically went no faster
My mind than is repined not while confessed;
At Hockey, cockey, golly, jolly good!
I used to mow about with mudded stick
At back position, wondering when Wood
Again might be attained for climbing trick:
The tallest tree we called The Monarch, and
From ninety-seven feet I Norfolk scanned.

Out and afar, the villages, the fields,
The ancient towers in their freestone might
And Blakeney Church espied, nigh moving wealds
Of grey and green and sapphire, from that height;
I'd sit there with a friend, we'd perch for hours,
Swaying as brothers, weighing what we thought
Of wasting Summertime sublime and powers
Of climbing forearm on that static Sport
Called Cricket! truly static for us both
Since, fielding, we would dream and make no runs
Batting – ah but, not to clambering loth
And one was wise, the other good at puns:
Punishment none for us because we were
At Nature Study, Bats, in belfry air!

Six miles or seven from the isling sea
My school stood set in beauty of her woods,
Benjamin Britten, Wystan Auden, me
And other mummers, number mongst her goods;
She may and she is fruitful even though
She writes my name in golden letters not!
She stood as I did come, as I did go
She stood, in fair far fields, a happy plot;
That Grasshopper which is the Gresham Crest
Has faithfully remained upon my mind
That hopefully can hop as can the best
Over the dilletante years behind:
I have not got one shadow of regret
Concerning Heyday light I won't forget.

N.B.
   If fit for publication this be felt
   Please note that *Dilettante* was mis-spelt!

Excelsior

First time I ever wrote a verse
Was on a ruined wall
At Baconthorpe, I might do worse
Than quote it – after all
This other stuff that has ensued
On eight and thirty years reviewed.

I quote aright, I cite the note
Made long ago to play the goat:

> Alas, alack, I am undone,
> I want to eat a currant-bun;
> But God is good, He told me so,
> The trees are swaying to and fro.

Would it be wise
To analyse
That silly-sounding thing?
I'd like to spell
Emmanuel
As Currant-bun: our King
In twofold eucharistic kind
Of grape and grain there reigns resigned,
If you will have it so;
Trees swaying to and fro
Could be the Springing from the Cross
O Hagios Athan-atos
A toss and two He took, and then,
Spread-eagled, soared and sent accord to men.

That ruined wall belonged to what
Was once a Priory, a plot
Blessed specially for praise, God ne'er forgot ...

Ritornello

At Monaco I spent a night
In Priory of Carmelite
And Monachus, remember, means a monk:
I went to bed at nine or ten
And looked towards that Gambling Den
And settled in a Cenobitic bunk,
But Monte Carlo is to me
No stronger than a cup of tea
Brewed-up to thrill but not to kill aboard a Junk.

As vagabond away I went
Having received The Sacrament
And after I had gladly broken fast
At courteous a Priory
As may be called a Friary ...
I crossed the border, climbed above the vast
Berippled beauty of that Sea
Which is creation's central glee
And up I went with heaven blent in attic cast.

Since it was fairly early still
A silence reigned upon the hill,
Atop of it a pantiled city gleamed:
Three hundred steps and maybe four
Had led me to the western door
Of Paradise, for Paradise it seemed ...
I saw one cat, one shabby man
Who proved to be a sacristan;
He cursed the cat, it spat at him and schemed
To enter in before the mouse
Came out from God's unopened House ...
For roaming cats and Roman Catholics redeemed.

Idyll of the Spring

Fontana di Clitumno,
Most crystalline of springs,
Where do the wildest roses blow?
Where widest grow the wings?
Since temple was to Venus set?
Beside your verdant marge
How many stood, would not forget
Thereafter where at large
They ever went,
With wonderment,
How limpid is the stream
That rises at Fontana di Clitumno like a dream?

Fontana di Clitumno
Still rises in my mind,
And all the hills of Umbria
Enthralling stand behind
And kindly too the angels stoop
And widest are their wings
And wildest are the roses there
Where recollection flings
Its fragrance up
Into the Cup
Of memory He holds
Who is the Father of us all, who calls us to the folds.

Fontana di Clitumno,
Is Venus not a star
Consorting with the ruined grace
Which halts the fastest car?
That linger may its human load
Beside the road to Rome
Recalling how the art of Greece
Became a part of home:
No halcyon,
No silver swan,
But would delight to be
Beside the stream while glides my theme with love of One in Three.

Fontana di Clitumno,
No goddess wantoning
Is Venus in fulfilment
But the Morning Star, I ween,
Yet better weans the best of Queens
From fetters of the world
Than all the centres of the scenes
Religious that are furled:
Astarte, startle never now,
Athene, leave thy loom,
Minerva wise, but rise and bow
To Wisdom in her womb.

Fontana di Clitumno,
I found you on a day
When I was whirled in via
Till we stopped upon the way
To graze at gracefulness gone by
Into a ruined fane
But glory founted at the spring
And history did reign;
No water-nymph descried we there,
No dryad fled to leaves
For Queen of Venus is my gain
And she is greeen of sleeves
Whose Lover is the Lord of light,
Whose Father is our own,
Whose Child is piping by the stream
All into One alone.

In magno silentio

Haunted by God The Holy Ghost from Prime
Till Compline and from Compline till the dawn
Being ridiculous is more sublime
Than being wise like pedants on the lawn
Forlornly arguing about the class
And genus of the daisies in the grass.

They say we'll push them up as we'll be down
Presently six good feet beneath God's turf
And that for each of us, whether a clown,
A king, a queen, a lawyer or a serf:
Below the surface shall our bodies lie
And rot, but shall our souls not be more high?

I saw a brainy head inside a glass
Jar and it jars upon me even now ...
Perhaps a pauper from the bottom class
Carried that head as high as he knew how
And so perhaps it was not such a brain
As Bertrand Russell had, but just a plain.

I begged a Priest to pray for all the folk
Whose bygone brains stand pickled on the benches
And neither did he think it was a joke
But took me seriously ... not like wenches
Disarming as a grocer's charming daughter
Who thought the courter's brain had caught the water.

Fraught with these melancholy thoughts I go
Weaving towards the twilight with my keys
And, suddenly recalling Pimlico
And Westminster Cathedral on my knees
In the confessional, I will rehearse
How I was overawed, in awful verse.

As sub-sub-sacristan, a simple wight
Determined to be coloured by the sun
Whenever I could get into its light,
I used to drain the cruets: more than one
Over the eight, on certain days were said
Seventy Masses there, some for the dead.

I quoted for the quiet of my mind
'Muzzle the Ox not as it treads the corn'
But conscience bid me presently to find
Confessor kindly as was ever born:
'I've swallowed such a lot of the remains'
I told him, and his golden answer reigns –

'There is a saying, Muzzle not the ox'
Said Michael Hollings from his hollow box!
No water wrought upon that giant brain
And, Master of Love's art, God's heart's his gain
And, not long after that which I record,
They made him Chaplain up at Oxenford.

Salve, San Antonio!

Finder of things
Both little and great,
Find me wide wings
To ascend to your state!
Tell me what words
For telling your power
Best befit birds that migrate to a tower:
Tower that leans
To listen so well,
Swallow my silence, ring swifly your bell!

First to narrate
A tale of a key
That none could trace
Till was given to me
The grace to enquire of Saint Anthony where
It might be enlocked to our shocking despair:
The house was Franciscan, the folk of it friars,
The key of the safe being lost made as liars
The people who said that their furniture had
Amongst it a safe, made the monks as if mad!

No good (they declared
As again there arose
Occasion to open
What wouldn't unclose):
No good? (I repeated) when each of us here
Is somewhat franciscan? our way is a clear,
Saint Anthony ask
And besiege him to show
Just where is the key we have fussed about so!

How often (they said)
We've prayed and in vain,
That key is a gone and will come not again!
All right (I replied)
I'll ask him anew
And then we shall see what'll genius do!
To breathe a petition
But briefly I kneeled
And then I arose and I smote
The safe crying,
Saint Anthony, yield!

Straightway on the top
Of the safe from a pile
There shook at my smiting the side of a file
And out of its shaking there came to a stop
The hiding of what we may style (on its drop)
A key to the castle of simple belief
That see can a Popery Saint through a papery sheaf:
The key had been hid for a period long
Enough to augment an Antonian song.

'God Shave the Queen!'

The fusty crowd,
The proud, the fat,
The dusty-browed
Belaboured cat
That crawled beneath the seething sounds
Of pariahs all, all dogs, no hounds
And right amidst the milling throngs
One Baboo sung that Song of Songs
But got it wrong though bright and keen
In pealing out: GOD SHAVE THE QUEEN!

However, if Our Lord and God
The son of Mary at her nod
Should shave His beard away He would
Be image of Our Lady good
For doubly is her like her Lamb
Whose Father is, as He, I AM.

God, Shave! ...... ! The Queen!

VI Alive with joy

Ornithological images

As peewits give their wills to wiles of wind
And lapwings wild to whimsies of the air
And kites Pan-African to where they'll find
Prey easily on outskirts of a flare;
As augur-buzzards give their ringing cries
To cupped upcurrents of an attic zone
And as a martial-eagle aptly flies
Over an area it calls its own;
As ravens watch for bright or tasty things
And jackdaws scotch the wardens of a church
Attempting to outwire aspiring wings
At belfry windows: so I'll end my search
A-tiptoe on the pinnacles of time
With chanticleer and contemplate – sublime!

Of swans

Companionable not, as ships that sail alone
With unhailed mast upon the vast unchartered sea
So is the single solitary swan to own
Tis never less alone, O Lord, than, throned with Thee,
Upon a pilgrimage where none but One can be.

Yet have I seen white swans in congregations great
Where pens and cobs and cobs and pens with cygnets go
In forceful concourse over Thames from gate to gate
Of Tower Bridge, from Waterloo at waters low
Towards the House of Lords and broads of Pimlico.

Weary were Thames unless bright swans might celebrate
With royal will those upper reaches preaching still
Sweet Solitude where woods and meadows recreate
Amidst the mind of each who'll find a silent thrill
Piping the panorama up from vale to hill.

From Birdlip I saw never one, but winds the Wye
Without they're in its current flowing on apace
Westward? whence, never Eastward may we turn our eye
Out and along, up, over ...? till our minds descry
A man that is immortal man by God's good grace
That shone upon the Swan of Avon's pensive face.

Here and there

Near as a word can get to birdclear sound
The martial-eagle's call is 'Kyrie!':
High-up it wheels, appealing round and round
To the Great Maker of the world's array
Of trees and grass and plants and seas and hay ...
So large a bird it is that out-of-sight
It almost never seems to get, what height!
High Yahweh's wings it wears with airy sway!

Aloft it wheels or stalls or stops suspended
And softly and more softly sounds its cry
Of 'Kyrie!': it is the Lord's most splendid
Talisman of the flight with which we'd vie
If only we might own upon the sly
A pair of rare rare wings with royal span
Appearing on the highest note which Pan
Can manage, Pan can manage ... Mighty Man!
And yet how lowly came that Piper nigh.

Nine Muses might attend upon that flyer
And blend with Him and send Him even higher:
Nimbly as Mercury a-tiptoe on
Thin air He's there, up there, in Erehwon!

Of ravens

Ravens are Yahweh's craftiness with wings,
They watch and pray to prey on unborn birds,
They steal like beggars but they feel like kings
And while they wheel they're too sublime for words;
They carry on like scavengers at will
Whose call is clearly not a clarion
But when they're crying over yonder hill
They make high concord with empyrean;
Lo and behold, their kind kept company
With bold Elias and Saint Benedict,
Frequenting Tower Hill they still descry
Napoleonic wartime being kicked:
    Tricked in to this by being on their side
    I look out quickly ... Up, O bliss, they glide!

Second vespers

A hundred cape-ravens and fifty again
Are over Chigona in joy
For Our Lady of Lourdes and their song is a plain
And their plan is to pool their employ.

Their only employ is in giving of praise
To Him who has fashioned the Hill
Where the rainbows are ready to rally their rays
Though the sunshine is riding the still.

There is barely a stir in the sentient air
Whose currents are secretly known
Albeit unfelt by the people whose prayer
Is never so loftily shown.

Cape-ravens are praying: the tips of their wings
Are given completely to One
Who victualled Elias by ravens, that kings
Might yet by the prophets be run.

The seers at their queerest are halcyon-fools,
The fools at their clearest are God's:
The earthling refuses His heavenly rules,
To the refuse He chooses He nods.

Had brave Bernadette seemed to nobody quaint
Her message had never been probed:
Today she is owned and enthroned as a saint
Whom black as a raven they robed.

Prime

A litle after five o'clock this morning
Came a loud volley from the honey-bees,
Peaceful complete invasion without warning
Taking possession of the bluegum trees;
Scarcely a breath of any breeze, grey sky
Trying for rainfall; liquid ringing note
Of a red-throated twinspot sounded, nigh
So far as might identify – my vote
Would hazard forty yards; the hum increased,
Resoundingly surrounded where I dwell,
Roseate flocks stole from the steely East
And hung, and listened to that lightsome bell:
    Blest tintinabulation, restful hum,
    Holding the still creation spellbound, dumb!

Nascent apiary

Bees like not to go out and to come in
By the same door – they care not to collide!
Though traffic is at certain times quite thin
This is a fundamental they decide;
They do not seek to be embroiled with dregs
Of coffee (which is poison unto them)
And yet they enter it, although one begs
Heaven to help them in their brief 'pro-tem';
Life of each individual that dwells
Within my lively dwelling in a hive
I cannot hope to measure, expert tells
That forty days at most boast bees alive;
    'In this short course which birth draws out to death'
    Would we might do as much, with such sweet breath!

'Leave me, O love that reachest but to dust
And thou, my mind, aspire to higher things ...' –
Whether Will Shakespeare was a beeman must
Be left to fancy on romancing wings;
If bees wrote sonnets they would show so stacked
With meaning and intelligence and zest
As ever even men most clever lacked
Backed by activity but half at best;
These are my golden days in which I mean
To grow in knowledge both of bees and God,
A swarm concentred warmly on its Queen
One Body is, at thirty thousand odd!
    Members of Christ that know God's heart and mind
    And share His good should not be hard to find.

Nocturne

The night-sound of a hive is like the fall
Of fairy raindrops on the tops of time
Or it is like the breeze in pine-trees tall
Or else like ocean's call to distant clime;
While eagle-owls may speak their spooky love
Wakefully scoring bullseyes each to each,
My thirty-thousand odd more godward prove
Humming and buzzing unatonic speech;
The night-sound of a hive alive with joy
At doing all for wooing one alone
Is like anticipation of a boy
Looking to summer-holidays he'll own:
    The night-sound of the hive amidst our cell
    Is less melodious than philomel
    But it is more harmonious as well.

'Quis ut Deus?'

A hive of bees is like one perfect being,
A colony of bees is like to God,
Their sound is compound and their airy seeing
Waits on the Queen whose will's their fairy rod;
To every hive its Queen is heart and mind
That pulses and directs amidst the whole
Whence more and more analogy I find
Bringing up bees from earth to heaven's soul;
A hive is Godlike in its unity,
A hive is like the Kingdom of a Queen
Who rules with Christ amidst the Trinity
Keeping each well-willed member blithe and keen:
A beehive is a universal wonder
Loving the sun, naught is more marvel under.

VII   *Neon-lights and ribbons*

A ballad of an ancient usher

Four thousand years before the birth of Christ
Adam lay bound to forfeit for his fall,
Freedom had wilfully been sacrificed
To knowing of the good and ill in all
And still revolved the unresolving ball:
The belle of it had been his Eve if she
Had hearkened not to Satan at his call ...
Who conquered and is conquered by a Tree?

Adam lay bound without the Eucharist
To free him in the Truth from evil's call,
Four thousand winters would not have sufficed
Had The Eternal Word not leapt time's wall
And settled for redemption of us all:
Through thirty nearly hidden years, through three
As clear as open-throated madrigal ...
Who conquered and is conquered by a Tree?

Our Father God The Thought begetting Christ
Who is His Word expressing Him in all
Was overcome with joy when, sacrificed,
Our Lord The King ascended to His Hall:
Rejoice, rejoice again, as saith Saint Paul
For death is swallowed up in Victory
So, through the Cross, arise and leap the Fall ...
Who conquered and is conquered by a Tree?

Envoi

Prince, if beneath the chestnut in the Fall
Of Autumn you played CONKERS as did we,
Gold Eden had old England's for its wall!
Who conquered and is conquered by a Tree?

Aubade

Ah, love is fed by gazing long
Upon that form and face
Which in appeal is far more strong
Than any other's grace,
But Love made Flesh on whom we look
Seems featurelessly round,
About Him lies the bell, the book,
Flies up the tinkling sound,
No babbling brook, no charming pool
Reflecting countenance to rule
Here runs or stands, and yet this thing
Is fairer than the fair:
Creation's King.

Could Jesus possibly have made
Himself more dimly traced?
It gleams but seems so unarrayed,
No head, no limbs, no waist!
O salutaris Hostia,
Innefably disguised,
We know exactly who you are,
The rest may be surmised:
The best of all in face and form
In sweet appealing honeyed swarm
My mind shall roll into a ball,
My heart shall sing this King
Fairer than all.

Encircled Lord, unboasting shape
Like nothingness agleam,
The fact is conned beyond escape,
We are like them that dream:
Behold, captivity is turned
Into our Triumph bright,
By us albeit quite unearned
We hail Him, Light of Light
And as, this Corpus Christi Day,
The sun swings up in glory gay
We thank our King for coming thus,
So marvelously small,
Oh All to us!

On the feast of Corpus Christi

We know the Body and the Blood of Christ
Are with us in His Holy Eucharist,
Since we believe it too we know He walks
In those receiving Him and through them talks
As peaceably to Mister Everyman
Whom they may meet and greet as Jesus can
But what we do not know is whether He
Remains and reigns this day in you and me
Since neither of us trusts the lusty sense
And both make simple Faith our sole defence
Against the demons who would put to rout
Our deep belief and true goodwill with doubt.

This is that happy morning when we feel
Safe on the rock while pealing steeples reel,
The rolling seas can never say us Nay
Because they mean MARIA: Hip hurray!
Mine Host is Landlord of the freest houses,
Throughout all Christendom our King carouses
And she who is His Barmaid has put on
Whatever dress best sends you to élan
And blends you in The Swan with Cob and Pen
That are Our Lord and Lady ... say Amen
To being Mistressed quickly as can ford
Through shallows of this page to deep accord.

Had you been there in Galilee of yore
And heard that Christ was three miles off or four
And that He was the whole expression rare
Of God who made the earth and gave the air
Would you have said that, since His Spirit is
Everywhere in His elemental guise,
You'd travel not a little way to see
The Word Incarnate? heard in Galilee
Jesus of Nazareth is in each tent
Where rests with us The Blessed Sacrament:
Worship the God of nature and do well,
Do better and adore Emmanuel.

Four Gospel-makers made His message clear,
Five wounds are in the Host as near as near,
Six senses you may have if you will ask
The Master kind who hides behind that mask
And sits amidst the Seven Sacraments
As Centre of them each in all those tents...
Eight modes Gregorian enchant the choirs
And muses nine are mine to sign the Shires
With Holy Cross: aspiring on the steeple
I'll chant it clearly for the chosen People
That He who is the Good from Nazareth
Is Perfect Jew, before and after death!

                    Alleluia, Shalom.

Cryptic chaplets

An angel came to second Eve and hailed,
Mary succeeded where First Eve had failed;
Our Lady hastened with Our Lord within,
The Baptist leapt where swept away was sin
Here is the House of Bread in every church,
Entered is Bethlehem nor far to search;
Rallies us all the Ark of God, and she
Offers us each in One to One in Three;
Elusive as migration of a bird
Laconic is the wisdom of the Word:
Lost for three days, upon the third was found
Even The Son whose Rising would resound.

The second Adam's garden-agony
Reflected from the Fall, whence rise would He;
Eve stole an apple, red as Christ became
E'en as they pealed the healing Fruit we claim;
Our Lady's Fruit stood robed in red and I
Followed the mob, my pride cried 'crucify!';
Like Tree of Life looked not that gaining Cross,
It felt far heavier than any loss;
Firmly the Tree was planted, whence The King
Entered the garden after suffering:
First Eve stole fruit, Our Lady's never stole
But twixt two thieves hung He who saves knave's soul.

The Triune Lord through Jesu's human form
Is become Ours, His heart has made us warm!
The garden where He rose keeps open gates
And, Holy Mass Christ's Rising celebrates;
Now see the Paschal Candle's parting cloud
In Christ's Ascent as blesses he the crowd;
A 'Veni, Sancte Spiritus' invites
Quickening Love to light our days and nights;
Untold is her Assumption? body, soul,
Eagle-Apocalypse descries her whole:
Eve's Queen is as each Ark that here contains
New Adam who abides with us and reigns.

Alleluia! Assumpta est!

Meridian

In sight of God man's life is panorama
Or else some much less beautiful display,
Whether he is a parson or a farmer
Or priest or least of coolies in Cathay
As from a hill our Maker will survey:
God will look down to see if he looks up
On equal terms with Jesu's loving Cup.

Behold, a chequered board: future and past
Run right and left of this our present time
Wherein is not irrevocably cast
Our fate if we vibrate with faith sublime
But mind our business well we must! the chime
Tells not again that hour upon this day
When known is what we do and think and say.

Our business is to get from earth to heaven
And help as many thither as we can,
Whether we dwell in Pakistan or Devon
Or Somerset, God won't forget to scan
As right and left unhid's to Him the plan
Royally instituted: to reject
Or to accept in Christ as God's elect.

The plan is that which brings us into line
With Christ The King whose Eucharist remains
Both to the right and left of where He'll sign
This as the very minute when He reigns
Provided that our hearts and hands and brains
Are lifted high to Him who came so low
From far above the Himalayan snow.

An early Christmas message

The whole wide world lay mightily depressed
At thought of the finality of death,
Since Eve and Adam failed the primal test
One line of hope did dimly shine: from Seth
Through Shem and Jesse led it down to Beth
Lehem at length, and there shines David's Star
Not dimly now to light the near and far.

The chorus of the angels and the pipes
Of shepherds on the starry Christmas scene
Are no less welcome to the guttersnipes
Than to the strong sequestered King and Queen;
Even the bourgeoisie may grow quite keen
And celebrate Christ's coming in their flats
With neon-lights and ribbons on their cats.

Some folk would rather celebrate The Word
Who is the full expression of The Thought
By being more unseen and more unheard
Now than at any other time: we sport
With silences and we shall not be caught
Outside our deepest solitude wherein
The Voice rejoices us afar from din.

Already it is nearly June: this Card
Will be in time ... I am an early bird!

Shalom and a very happy Christmas!

VIII   *Forth on pilgrimage*

'In principio'

In the beginning God created heaven,
In the beginning God created earth,
He took His time about creating Devon,
E'en Switzerland sublime was but a dearth
In the beginning: formless, void, unbright
Till God expressed His thought – 'Let there be light'.

The Father's thought was in the Word before
It was, in the beginning, so expressed;
'Let there be light' was, being said, the door
Whereby came warmth and beauty and the rest:
The Father's thought expressed was clearly heard
When light went forth with Christ the Son, the Word.

Chaos and darkness, formlessness and void
Gave way with all their nothingness to light,
The deep awoke from sleep and much enjoyed
Gazing amazed at raising of the height:
The Father said what always He had thought,
'Let there be light, My Son, as One we'll sport!'.

The Spirit moved upon the waters' face
And proved Himself in brooding like a bird,
Whether a dove or halcyon we trace
Graceful imagination's not absurd;
The Father is the Thought, the Word's the Son
The Spirit is the Voice and Three are One.

The firmament bears witness to the light,
The firmament (and heaven is its name)
Is not (although when hued in blue so bright)
Itself the light, the sun, the ball of flame:
The Baptist, not himself the Lord of all,
Bore witness bright, as sky to lighting ball.

Six verses lead in Genesis and six
In Gospel Fourth to Faith of Christendom,
Reflects God's Son His 'Dei Genitrix'
And shines in darkness drowning not the sum:
Between the Dispensations John spake clearly,
The merry sky is heaven very nearly!

Exploiting space get grace the nations may
To find God's Kingdom near, not far away.

Brewing

First Eve fell fast for fallen fiend's false fable,
Foul weather followed for us folk forlorn,
Cain was our forefather and slain lay Abel,
Limped lame the aching line till Seth was born;

Our call became to be the sons of God
Who talked to Enos and with Enoch walked,
Obeyed was Heaven's peremptory nod
And Hell felt shame and Satan's claim was baulked;

Seth's line then intermingled with the rest
And saw how fair men's daughters had become
Though only Noah's line survived the test
Knight-errant out of Ur would stir the drum:

> Abram stood forth, the Patriarchs were grounded
> Slowly in faith, low trump on Sinai sounded.

Miriam danced upon the homeward shore
And took a timbrel for her Namesake shining,
The Son of Man whose Love fulfils the Law
Sat still amidst His seers God's will divining;

The ram in Dan that battled with the goat
Declared 'I El am Paschal to the brim!',
Almighty Pan the Lord piped Abel's note
In Ancient Greece and goaled with peaceful hymn;

I AM put golden fleece of Miriam on
And Second Eve, having believed those tidings,
Brought forth the Word-made-flesh and God did don
Man's body, banning him from old backsliding:

> Even as AVE Eva's name reverses
> So we are sown in blessings and not curses.

Far from the Garden foremost parents wended
And primal bearers of our fallen race
Bore weather wild with milder weather blended
Nor mended much till grace's call we trace;

We trace it back to Enos and to Enoch
And tracing it we face the Lord of Hosts
Till Summer's pastorale o'ercomes the pibroch
Of skeerling Winter with its hinter boast;

Then left behind lie wildernesses bleak
And long outdated is the song of sand,
Our lineage is Hebrew, Latin, Greek
As, Lamb-led flock, on Roman Rock we stand:

Gethsemane looks through to Easter-Garden
And Eden Now is sunlit with true pardon.

'Fear no more the heat of the Sun'
For He is God and we are One
In Him with Triune Love we toast
As Father, Son and Holy Ghost
Who are The Thought, The Word, The Voice
Of Love: One Lord... so run, rejoice
That 'the furious winter's rages'
Are annulled and mulled by stages!
Forth on pilgrimage we go
Unwrathfully with A and O.

Vigil of All Saints, 1978

63

Untearfully at Tierce

Bidden by God to multiply in Eden
They did it out as exiles in the wild,
No graceful traces there of that fair garden
But Abel was a smooth and comely child;
The elder and the younger persevere
In contest and in contrast through the ages,
The choice of love rejoices, casts out fear
After terse struggles in the awkward stages;
And so goes Isaac forward with his father,
And so goes Joseph onward with the ass
And Brother Jacques, bemused by brooks, would rather
There meditate but not be late for Mass:
   Hosanna is the Tenor of the peal
   That sways the spires and makes the steeples reel.

Unfearfully at Sext

The Abbey down at Buckfast bears a Bourdon,
Weighs seven tons at least that priestly Bell
Which never is a swung but struck like Jordan
To let the friends go through though foes to fell;
Boxing with martinets twill not fox martyrs,
It rings for truth so sooth it puts to flight
And though we patter, clatter on like carters,
The Pater Noster reigns in our delight;
Martyrs were ground like wheat and tried like silver
On earth whence now in heaven they are goaled,
Bright salmon leap shalomming from the river,
Right monks psalm on enchanting as of old:
   Sad gates of hell would see glad banners furled
   So marvel not if hates you here the world.

Cheerfully at None

Struck on the one cheek swiftly turn the other,
Swallowing down your wrath you'll swallow his
Up quickly and improve your sickly brother
Without reproving him while temper flies;
I migrant am and migrant are you not?
Our big reward is broader than the sea,
Play cool until you rule your anger hot
And we'll roucoule like doves with ungloved glee;
If thieves will think our shirts well worth the stealing
Then after them we'll run to give them pants!
Adhere to Truth as flies do to the ceiling,
Walk upsidedown like clowns whilst frowning rants!
       Should you go over-Sext more fast than most
       Buxom's the Barmaid of Mine Highest Host.

It's closing-time already, two o'clock ...
We'll open-up for Evensong, old cock!

Evensong

Now even grow we all in one sweet song:
Magnificat, so THAT was not too long!

Quid nunc?

Why is there music in my heart?
What is the music of the spheres?
How did Ludwig hear his art
With naught but deafness in his ears?
O whence is this deep certainty
And whither will it bound?:
Harmony is silence of a melody
And silence is the harmony of sound.

This certainty was well instilled
In him on whom I meant to build
An edifice as different
From Babel as is elephant
From ant; and high upon a hill
I'll standfast
Like a radar-mast
And still. ...

My mast is up on Roman Fell
Close to The Cross and Mary's Well,
My station on the Pennine Chain
At zenith I take up again;
My notion is a very good
And no commotion be there should:
The night is clear, the stars are bright,
Moon will appear and steer aright.

Stylite, sermonize;
Xenophon, stylize;
Close eyes, Xenophobe,
Ostracize the trot-globe!

Yield, thou letter last but one,
On Alpha bet
As being Omega's own son
And End shall never set:
Give, vibrate, penultimate,
Till all is Zed and done save Zen. ...
I oscillate?

Ouija – pass me it!
Elijah, wait a bit,
You came again in Baptist, did you not?
If we will haver then
And doodle with our Zen
We may as well let Israel be the spot:
Let Carmel be the part
Got nearest to the heart
Of God who matters most –
Mine Host, art coming?
'When I shall come I will,
My Church is Roman still
Whither leads Jewish Street' ... the wires are humming!

The Queen Bee's Knees
With a live-wire's ease
Move rhythmically, lightly;
She croons to the crowd, 'Now leave Us, please'
And this incites, thrice brightly,
Quiet to keep
At the foot of the steep
Of the hill called Roman Fell
Whither there climb
At the present time
Folk of Emmanuel,
For the Jewish Street
Goes up to greet
Where meets with Holy Rome
The Hebrew core of the evermore
In Jerusalem New, True Home:
Our Home, indeed,
Of Abraham's seed ...

Glows Miriam Moon, 'Close to me!'.

Ad tertiam

I will relate all Thy wonders,
I will be glad and rejoice!
Thou art the God of the thunders
Yet Thine is the still small voice:
After the whirlwind and after the fire
Thine is the laughter, the light and the lyre!

IX   *Shalom, Mashonaland*

Chigona

There is a hill, not far away
And more a gray than green;
But it is warm, its granite gay,
Way to the Fairy Queen!

So near it stands that evermore
Is at my lintel now,
Eternity is at my door
So low that I must bow:

I bow to Him who made this earth
So exquisitely fair,
I bow to her by whom his worth
Had birth in Winter air.

Sing Heigh for summer never seems
To end or ebb away!
Sing Ho for Shepherdess of themes
High on her hilltop, Fay!

By moonlight

I rose with a shout –
I'll strike it out
(I cried), that shortfall tale
Shall long for me to grow strong in glee
As the moonlit nightingale!
So I quickly dressed and climbed the hill
'Chigona' called: an enthralling still ...

There was hardly a sound
For the night lay bound
In the light-spell, moon and stars;
Soft freedom leapt
For the folk that slept,
On the drums of nears and fars
In the drinking band of Mashonaland
Who count no yoke
But a fitting joke
Their all-night sit or stand ...

I ran round a track at the top
For a dozen times
And did not slack or stop
To plan my rhymes ...

I returned and chanticleer cried,'To-bed!' –
Hark, what an odd remark
For you! (I said).

Kraaldom

Rolling off from the edge of time
I'll stroll Mashonaland in rhyme
Confining me to a span that rolls
From here to the Mission of All Souls:
Three days ago and nearly four
I walked ten miles to heaven's door.

The cocks crow thrice and again they crow
And the dawn is over my goal aglow,
Like a bended bow the crescent moon
Aims at my Dame Aurora ... soon
The East is aflame; and the Western Hill
Is the cloister-wall of my calling still.

Mootamewa's ancient arid bulk
Towers ahead – no glowering sulk
But a powered orientating cry
From time towards eternity:
... And at half-past nine o'clock or so
Last Friday morn I forth did go.

The Kraals were neat and the garners clean,
Each headman's wife was a lively Queen,
I felt that I'd known their homes since first
Adam's fall was an unaccurst
And the heart and mind of Mashonaland!
Trod East in the glee of God: re-manned!

Where the baobab trees loom large and oft
Had I worn a hat that hat I'd doffed
As I saw the height and the house divine
Of All Souls Church in the light ashine:
The heat was great in the gate of noon
But my heart was elate and I'd get there soon ...

A drunken youth had assured my track
An hour ago and a four-miles back,
Jerusalem reeled in the noonday sun
And the high land pealed for the low land won
And I got there then to a Latin home
In Mashonaland on the path to Rome!

Veritas, sed in vino not,
Spaghetti I had and a coffee hot
And fast two more and a welcome there
Which spells Rome mellow, everywhere:
The kraals stood back and their kings and queens
Smiled in the good of the God of peaceful scenes.

Little world of Dunlopillo

This little world is insulated well
Against the shocks of politics and pride,
Smaller than all Mashona towns you'd tell,
Taller than leaders mean of lofty side;
Its slavery to fashion but consists
In taking gratefully whatever comes
By way of free apparel, up its fists
At fate it puts not, fingers lacks and thumbs;
Were I to measure out its breadth and length
It might be something like three hundred yards
Broad by five hundred long, the Lord's its strength
And it abounds in many kinds of cards:
I'll play no more than four hereon and start
With one nigh sightless minstrel, light of heart.

This mellow fellow lacks for fingers not
And uses them to play that little harp
Called 'Mbira' in the Shona tongue, he's got
A voice melodious and no tone sharp;
Twice he is married, both his wives are here,
Veronica and Agnes – he is Paul
Kwangwari and he comes from not so near
As many, Wankie's rather far from call;
In stature he is large, in movement slow,
To merriment he's pleasurably quick,
His heart is very warm, his art is so
Sequestered that to hear it needs a trick
Of coming softly to his hut: no sham
At all in Paul, whose nearest call is Jam.

Jam Jonson's sight is reasonably good,
His totem is the Lion and his head
Is handsome, somewhat leonine one could
Call it, a trifle grizzled, he's not wed;
He loves to sit and not to think too much,
Often he wears for hat a rakish straw,
He always greets one with a smile of such
Benevolence it cheers one to the core;
His door stands out amongst the other portals
As being extra solid, extra new,
The wood of it came down amongst us mortals
From Salisbury (as packing-case in lieu):
Jam sits amidst his kitchen like a lord
Who fits the pattern of our humour broad.

Jam was no sticky business to describe
But I am almost at a loss to tell
(Apart from name and totem, sex and tribe)
Clearly of her who next to Jam doth dwell;
She daily follows doggedly until
Her grogginess achieves me and a pill
In which persistence she is not surpassed
Except by Naomi (the neighbour next
But one to ill Maria), and this last
Of four shall make no more my score a vext:
Naomi's totem is a Monkey, she
Sets all her antics upon aspirins
Of which if daily I supply her three
She gets her equilibrium, and grins!

All square – this lilting world of Done Lopilloes
May class our mighty waves of pains light billows;
Its donjon is the presence of the Lord,
Its fortress is its art of heart's accord;
Its song is oft such dissonance to ears
Attuned to pure polyphony for years
That I should make mine shorter, bray the less
And pray the more: hee-haw, brave wilderness!

Momento Kahoto

This day died one more John 'ere clear the dawn
Was chanted by the cocks that rock the roosts
But all did not fall flat though unforlorn
None showed themselves and custom got its boosts;
So stumps were clasped by stumps and shaken duly
For loss of him whose last ten months had been
A sort of walking death with breath that truly
Breathed no despairing air upon our scene;
No, John Kahoto is a brave man gone
Over the Styx to where he need not burn
Any more firewood... awful thin grew John
And felt the cold too keenly in his turn:
    Blind Peter, whom I bathed at two o'clock,
    Said sorry slowly, fast reviewed his stock.

Susanna's now a clocking hen on twelve
Eggs that increased from eight in four full days,
Kahoto has gone forth the world to shelve
Where golden silence silver speech allays;
Remember we long John, so thin of shank,
And pray that he may win the pleasant fields
Far and away beyond the grave gone dank
And high above what earthly harvest yields;
John loved his garden and his growing cobs
And, almost to the end, he'd potter forth
To see what in his land might offer jobs...
He'd totter o'er the road, look South and North:
    If there's no Jacaranda Avenue
    In heaven, John, odds on no meeting you!

Josephite

In such a night as rarest dreams are made on
I lay awake and thus was wakened not
When came, upon the door of this my donjon,
A peremptory knocking, dot dot dot;
Bright was the moon and shining high to East
And she who'd knocked stood almost at the brink
Of childbirth and anxiety increased
Since locked lay telephone – no time to think
For long, no time to wink at circumstance,
No telephoning for the ambulance ...
I thought 'wheel-chair', deliberating ceased.

The winding uphill road, ashine in dust,
Showed not its most cooperative face,
The transport was indeed a bare needs-must
Slowed by the dusty road, but gleamed there grace
In moonlight as I asked the lady's name
And, faintly, 'Mary' for an answer came.

We reached the hospital (but two miles hence)
And ready hospitality thereat
Amidst those hours we call 'the small' lay dense
In summer slumber – we did not come pat pat!
At last appeared that watchman Brother James
Whose air was not aware of urgent claims.

The lady I delivered to a bed,
If yet she is delivered of her child
I know not: to occasion I was wed
But after me the babe may not be styled ...
The lady's name was Mary and I think
Hereby my own with Joseph's one may link.

Paradise tossed aside: 'Incipit lamentatio ...'

Here in Mashonaland, God's dwindling park
Where fragrant cherries wild bloom white midst crowns
Of red masasas, looms now large a dark
Dragonlike Axe with many heads that downs
Badly good woods in lumps, leaves stumps to rot
Blackened by fires, by bulbul-choirs forgot.

Lest this lament should seem insipid, take
As starting-point I only one great kraal
And that's a leper-camp where, for the sake
Of terror of the Snake, they root up all
Attempts of grass to grow, and this despite
Handicaps on the left and on the right!

Salt of the earth in many ways, in this
These lepers are no wiser than the rest
Of Shona Kraaldom, scenery like bliss
Is swept aside with deft defiant zest!
Twould seem the ancient fiend in serpent's shape
Has won the desert by the garden's rape.

Here in Mashonaland, where orioles
With liquid notes make haloes for the Spring,
Is all the score for war-memorials
And why then still do bulbuls trill and sing?
The Axe presents the Hammer and the Sickle
With fellow promise never to be fickle.

Sever the forests, limb by limb, from heaven
And sharply bring them down flatlong to earth
So that your habitat, with hell for leaven,
May crave the Brave New World for all its worth
Of knavish tricks that gird against The King
Whose Tree still stands where axe and hammer ring.

Is it for fear of snakes and lasting dread
Of Eden's serpent that they scour the land
Clean of each blade of grass, to show its head
So keen? keen winds shall blow on scene of sand
Swept willy-nilly into eyes and chests
Of this mad race that graces glad arrests!

Attests that Garden to the mind of God
But their desserts are Desert as they hack
Since, all along each track Prince Shona's trod,
The trunks are slashed, the branches are bent back
Or severed...nay, not even for their fires
Nor for odd posts to prop their toppling byres.

'Byres' is as homely as I'll get in telling
Such savage wantonness, such random felling.

So many think that heaven is a slab
Of concrete! now in both the hemispheres
The mind of petty man has got so drab
That there's no love therein to cast out fears
Of viruses and microbes, snakes and worms:
Take we Hell's diet on the Devil's terms!

Else it is greed, for money and for land,
That makes a desert of God's wide wild Eden;
When I was young a Heronry did stand
With three-score nests and ten twixt earth and heaven:
It stood in Norfolk near King's Lynn until
Cut down to grow potatoes: growing still?

Man is a vandal and a beastly thing
Where'er his ears are deaf to Pan's sweet piping,
Yet he was set as viceroy to King
Eternal once: oh may this dunce's typing
Re-stir the springs of immortality
And may my wit befit eternity.

As gentle and unwarlike as the Shona
May seem to earthbound beings on two legs
He is not fit a bit to be the owner
Even of one odd acre: whose eggs
Him on to getting of good land should tax
Unyieldingly his wielding of the axe!

The snake has triumphed over Africa,
Can Pan not pipe it to renounce its gain?
For fear of snakes they sweep the near and far
Clear of all grass that grows: greedy for grain
Of sterile sand and barren rock, they bring
Down to a desert bare fair nature's fling!

Hark, this amongst the gentle lepers: one,
Who calls his own at least four acres, found
That two most fruitful mangoe-trees kept sun
Off from his maize and razed them to the ground!
Such ravin, for the sake of mealie-cobs
Maybe ten more, on this my score sets nobs.

The sun shall glare on thee, unshining Shona,
Of moonscape only, Goat, be gloating owner!

They hate the flowers and they loathe the blooms,
Wild cherry-trees in blossom make them writhe,
Barren their brides are not but hot! their brooms
Bear away beauty: booty for the scythe
Is each green blade of grass in reach, they are
Grooms that graze nightmares on this lightsome star.

Their destiny must be to stoke the fires
Where there are greenwoods none, no sun, no choirs!

The Shona patience shines not in this war
Brightly as might attribute it to Christ,
The Matabele saw its like before
When here were neither Church nor Eucharist:
Frail apathy in face of whirling woes
Hails not The Cross that still stands still and glows.

To honour of their titulary Saint
Ignatius were men loyal when guerillas
Threatened because, upon the face, the paint
So rightly white gave nightblack knaves the shivers?
That status, by those 'faithful', was destroyed
Utterly and the mutterers deployed.

Unstable Boys, Aunt Mabel ruled you well
And set you to the garden with the hose
And if you squirted it at Clarabel
Over the fence it kept her on her toes
Till soon, at heat of noon, you two would weave
Together, yes, and never wish to leave!

Far better be at that than hacking down
The 'Nyama-ropa' with its flesh and blood
Or else than laying waste the woodland-crown
As far from Town as Justice from M'Llud
Who sentenced you to hanging for your tricks
So heavily involved in Politics.

Let us salute the shades of bootless fellows
Who stole the fruit whence bad o'erwhelmed the good!
Well Bottom wove, well Flute did mend the bellows
But 'Fudza-mombé' felled not well the wood
Since, starveling prince, he left the ragged stumps
Looking like jagged scarecrows in the dumps.

Their sole desire is body's sustenance,
Main inspiration of their souls is maize,
Their minds lie fallow to the foe's advance
With tales of fellowship, fools in a haze
Of brash transistors, high-heeled shoes and prams
They skip towards that Russian Bear like lambs!

Daleth hath dalliance with Dillitanté,
Hies to Dry-Cleaners He three times a week
And both of them have got a book on Danté,
Of both of them tis better not to speak
Since neither of them knows two words in Greek:
Kyrie éleison.

Unstable Boys, Aunt Mabel ruled you well
And though mine English Aunt was not the rage
Bad Cain enables you for naught but Hell,
For cabbages is all your pilgrimage:
Shalom, Mashonaland? such greeting good
Will but come back as ill, still hacking wood.

X   Envoi

Beedom attained

A stronghold for my verses is become
What long I have intended for a hive,
Bees may inspect it and about it hum
But for an entry now they should not strive;
Whether their honey is a better thing
Than my unpublished poetry depends
Only on the opinion of the King
Of heather, lime and rhyme, and verse which blends;
I am contented that my verse should stay
Unread, unlooked at, unrespected, dumb
Until the time when that same King shall say
'Now let the world with these unfurled go hum!'
    Then shall all this, all these, my verse entire
    Or only partly, hear God's 'Go up higher'.